美国宪法

How We Organize Ourselves | Non-Fiction Series

Copyright © 2022 by Level Learning, INC. and Washington Yu Ying PCS™
Original and Edited Text Copyright © 2022 by Washington Yu Ying PCS™

All rights reserved. No part of this book in whole or part may be reproduced without written permission from the publisher.

Published by Level Learning, INC.
Content Contributors:
Washington Yu Ying PCS™ - Jianhua (Allen) Zhong, Pearl Zao He You
Level Learning - Jingyao Qi

Illustrations by: Josh Taira

Leveling classification based on Level Learning standard.
For full description, visit www.levellearning.com

ISBN 978-1-64040-115-0
Simplified Chinese Edition

About Level Learning™:
Level Learning provides a literacy focused curriculum specifically designed for K-12 Chinese as a Second Language classrooms. Our program offers 20 levels of specific and detailed objectives, leveled texts and passages, mastery-based online assessment, and analytics to enable data-driven instruction. Level Learning reading curriculum for both literature and informational text emphasize grammar and comprehension skills to help teachers develop confident and independent Chinese language readers. The non-fiction series of books are specifically designed to support our informational text course based on multiple national standards. To learn more about our entire offering, visit www.levellearning.com.

About Washington Yu Ying PCS™:
Washington Yu Ying PCS is a Mandarin English dual language immersion International Baccalaureate (IB) World school. Yu Ying's mission is to inspire and prepare young people to create a better world by challenging them to reach their full potential in a nurturing Chinese/English educational environment. Yu Ying's comprehensive IB, dual immersion curriculum equips students with global competencies for success in the real world. As a leader in immersion education, Yu Ying is determined to advance Chinese language programs and global citizenry education by helping other schools create and strengthen their Chinese programs. For more information, email: products@washingtonyuying.org

美国宪法是美国的最高法律，是在1788年被通过的。美国人民都要遵守宪法的规定。

CONSTITUTION
宪法

THE U.S. CONGRESS
国会

THE WHITE HOUSE
白宫

THE SUPREME COURT
最高法院

LEGISLATIVE
立法

EXECUTIVE
行政

JUDICIAL
司法

宪法规定：美国有国会、总统和最高法院。

CONSTITUTION
宪法规定

THE U.S. CONGRESS
国会

THE WHITE HOUSE
白宫

THE SUPREME COURT
最高法院

国会制定法律,总统执行法律,法院诠释法律。

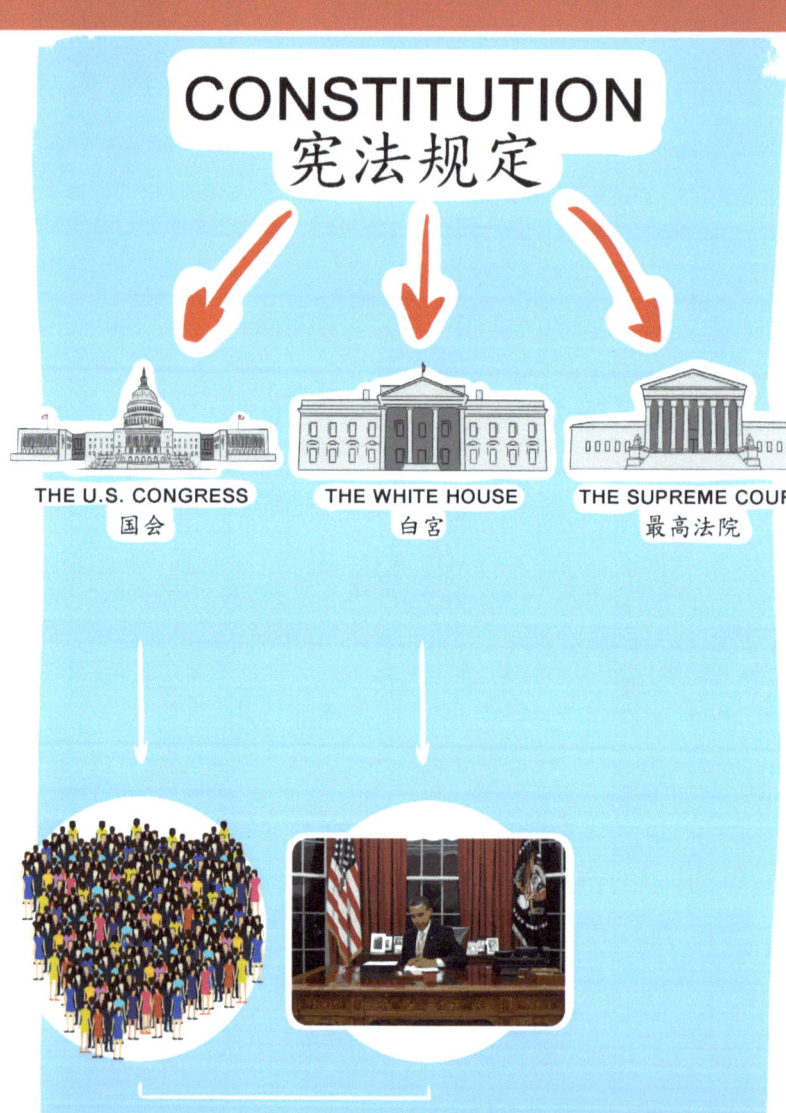

美国的国会由议员组成。美国的总统和议员由选举产生。

国会可以修正宪法，被修正的宪法叫作宪法修正案。到2017年为止，美国宪法一共有27条宪法修正案。修正案的第一条到第十条也叫权利法案。

BILL OF RIGHTS
权利法案

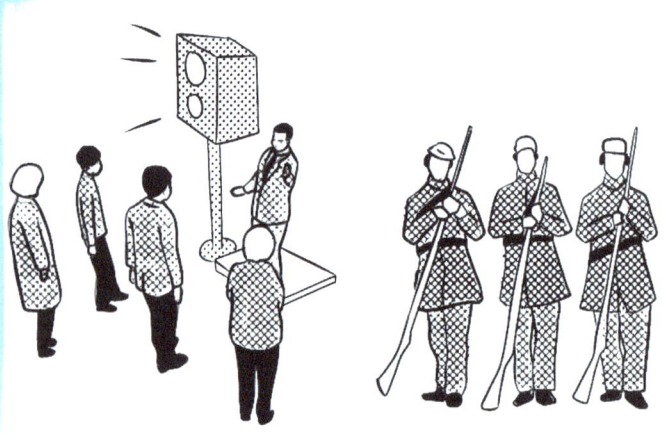

权利法案保护美国人民的权利。比如，人们有表达看法的权利，人们有参加宗教活动的权利等等。

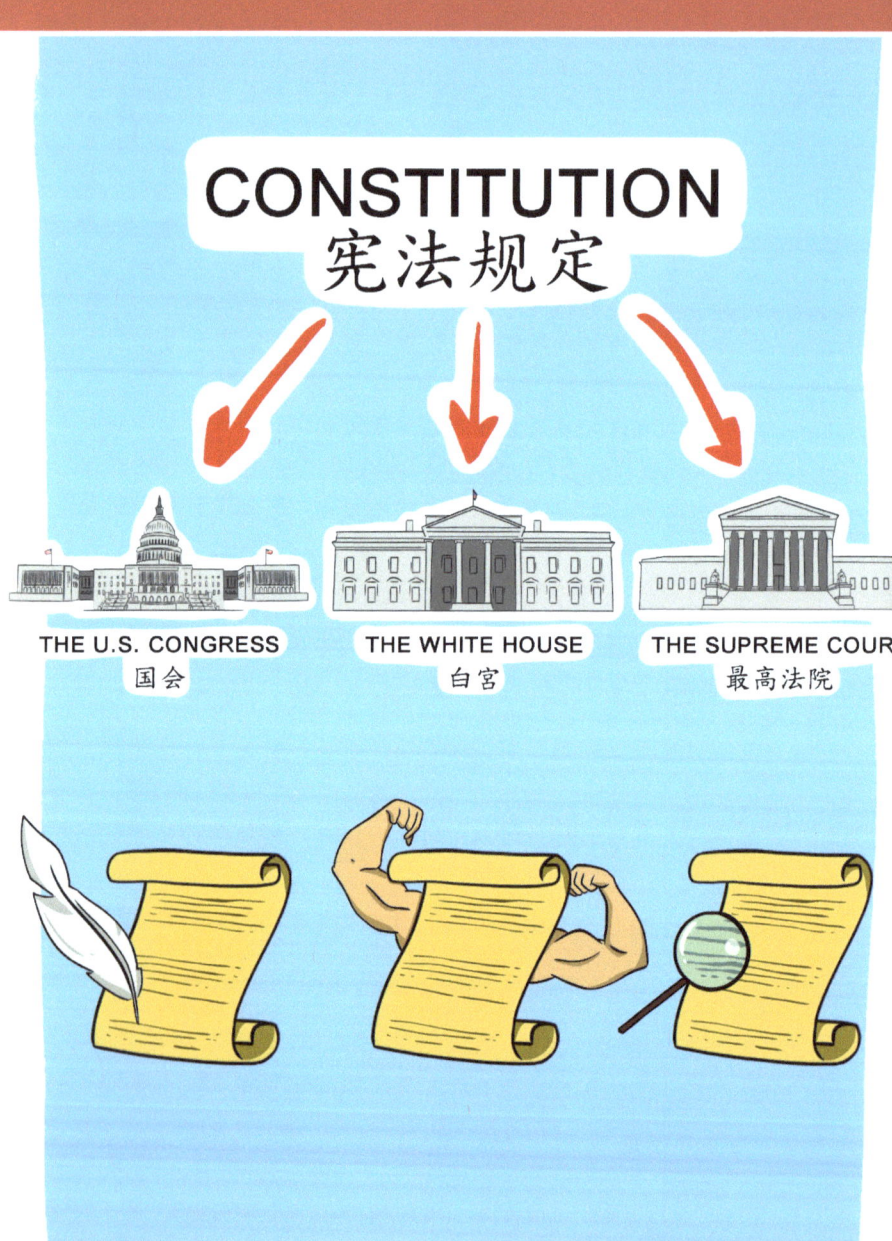

今天的美国还在使用之前的宪法。

Glossary

	Pinyin	English Definition
宪法	xiàn fǎ	constitution
法律	fǎ lǜ	law
遵守	zūn shǒu	to comply
规定	guī dìng	rule, provision
国会	guó huì	Congress
总统	zǒng tǒng	President (of the U.S.)
法院	fǎ yuàn	court
制定	zhì dìng	to make (law)
执行	zhí xíng	to enforce
诠释	quán shì	to interpret
由	yóu	by
议员	yì yuán	member
组成	zǔ chéng	to form
选举	xuǎn jǔ	to elect

	Pinyin	English Definition
修正	xiū zhèng	to amend
修正案	xiū zhèng àn	amendment
权利法案	quán lì fǎ àn	Bill of Rights
权利	quán lì	rights
参加	cān jiā	to participate
宗教	zōng jiào	religion
活动	huó dòng	activity

www.ingramcontent.com/pod-product-compliance
Lightning Source LLC
Chambersburg PA
CBHW041226070526

44584CB00001B/116